Schwerpunktthema

Abitur Englisch

The Day After Tomorrow

A Film Study

Cornelsen

The Day After Tomorrow: A Film Study

von Christina Diehr und Cordula Rohlmann-Reineke

Verlagsredaktion

Ingrid von der Felsen-Ferguson

Layout und technische Umsetzung

May + Steinmüller, Designbureau, Berlin

Umschlaggestaltung

havemannundmosch, bureau für gestaltung, Berlin

www.cornelsen.de

1. Auflage, 1. Druck 2011

Alle Drucke dieser Auflage sind inhaltlich unverändert und können im Unterricht nebeneinander verwendet werden.

Druck: CS-Druck CornelsenStürtz, Berlin

ISBN 978-3-06-032512-2

Inhalt gedruckt auf säurefreiem Papier aus nachhaltiger Forstwirtschaft.

Contents

ACKNOWLEDGEMENTS

Texts: p. 19 Songtext: It's not time to make a change, by Cat Stevens, © Cat Music Ltd. / EMI Music Publishing Germany GmbH & Co. KG, Hamburg; p. 27 ff. The Day After Tomorrow: Interview with Roland Emmerich, by Todd Gilchrist, www.blackfilm.com, May 2004 (c) 2004 BlackFilm.com; p. 31 ff. A lot of hot air – A scientist's view, by Patrick J. Michaels, 24 May 2004 (c) 2004 USA TODAY, a division of Gannett Co. Inc.; p. 34 The Day After Tomorrow – Film review, by Movie Gazette, www.movie-gazette.com, 26 February 2004 (c) © Web Gazette LLP

Illustrations: Cover: all images from: Fotolia (Statue of Liberty # 28271194: © vlad_g, Statue of Liberty # 27953931: © vlad_g, Mountains: © Werner Büchel, Icicles: © Gentoo Multimedia, Ice crystal: © mirpic; pp. 5, 16, 17, 20, 21, 22, 23, 25, 26: all stills from: The Day After Tomorrow, 2004, a film by Roland Emmerich, © 2004 Twentieth Century Fox Film Corporation; p. 4 © Vhrsti / www.toonpool.com p. 13 left © Cinetext Bildarchiv, middle © Cinetext / Sammlung Richter, right © 20th Century Fox / The Kobal Collection, p. 14 all icons from: Shutterstock images (Action Films: © John Young, Adventure Films: © Likiyanova Natalia / frenta, Biographical Films: © Shako, Chick Films: © superdumb, Comedy Films: © argus, Crime and Gangster Films: © robodread, Detective Films: © Tonis Pan, Disaster Films: © SergeyDV, Drama Films: © Alexander A. Sobolev, Epic and Historical Films: © Maugli, Fantasy Films: © Linda Brotkorb, Film Noir: © Helea, Guy Films: © wtamas, Horror Films: © rudall30, Musical and Dance Films: © James Thew, Melodramas: © Adam Tinney, Science Fiction: © Tim the Finn, Road Films: © trekandshoot, Romance Films: © photostockar, Sports Films: © Anna Fraitova, Supernatural Films: © Boguslav Mazur, Thriller: © Nitipong Ballapavanich, War/Anti-War Films: © karlovserg, Western: © Jana Guothova; p. 36 top © Nick Kim / www.CartoonStock.com, bottom Mind Map "Combating global warming", © S. Genovese / www.learningfundamentals.com.au

Liebe Schülerinnen und Schüler,

in diesem Arbeitsheft möchten wir Ihnen unterschiedliche Zugangsmöglichkeiten zu dem Film *The Day After Tomorrow* eröffnen, der bei seinem Erscheinen im Jahr 2004 sehr viele Zuschauer ins Kino lockte.

Dem Thema des Films, dem Aspekt der globalen Erwärmung, kann man sich heutzutage nur schwer entziehen: Sämtliche Medien berichten in unterschiedlichen Formaten darüber. Immer wieder wird insbesondere in der letzten Zeit auf die negativen Folgen der globalen Erwärmung hingewiesen. Von Wissenschaftlern wurde bereits in mehreren Modellrechnungen vorhergesagt, dass durch die globale Erwärmung das arktische Eis schmilzt, dann in den Atlantik fließt und den sogenannten Tiefenwasserstrom im Nordatlantik urplötzlich versiegen lässt.

Im Film geht es um genau diese Folgen globaler Erwärmung. Zugleich werden unterschiedliche zwischenmenschliche Beziehungen thematisiert, bei denen die Vater-Sohn-Beziehung eine besondere Rolle einnimmt. Darum haben wir auf diesen Aspekt ein besonderes Augenmerk gelegt.

Das Arbeitsheft ist so angelegt, dass Sie sich den Film mit seinen vielfältigen Inhalten selbstständig erschließen können. Dabei sind wir nicht chronologisch, sondern thematisch vorgegangen.

Nach einer ersten Einführung in die Filmhandlung können Sie sich mittels einiger *pre-viewing activities* auf den Filminhalt einlassen und Mutmaßungen über den genaueren Verlauf anstellen.

Die folgenden *while-viewing-activities* können in der im Heft vorgeschlagenen Reihenfolge oder auch in beliebiger Abfolge bearbeitet werden. Hier wird besonderer Wert darauf gelegt, den Einsatz spezifisch filmischer Mittel zu verfolgen. Dabei sollte Ihnen das gängige Vokabular der Filmanalyse vertraut sein. Sie können hierzu das Worksheet ▸ *Selected terms for film analysis* unter www.cornelsen.de/abi-e (dort das *A Day After Tomorrow*-Cover anklicken) hinzuziehen.
Eine zentrale Rolle spielt bei der Filmanalyse natürlich auch, die zugrunde liegenden Intentionen der Figuren herauszuarbeiten und kritisch zu hinterfragen. Dies geht im Arbeitsheft zum Teil mit kreativen Schreibaufträgen einher.

Das Erzeugen und Erleben von Spannung spielt bei einem Film wie diesem eine sehr wichtige Rolle – und damit verbunden natürlich auch der Einsatz von *special effects*. Aus diesem Grund haben wir Wert darauf gelegt, dass besonders spannungsgeladene Szenen Gegenstand einer genaueren Analyse sind.

The Day After Tomorrow
(2004)

Directed by	Roland Emmerich
Writing credits	Roland Emmerich, Jeffrey Nachmanoff
Produced by	Roland Emmerich, Mark Gordon

Cast

Jack Hall	Dennis Quaid
Sam Hall	Jake Gyllenhaal
Laura Chapman	Emmy Rossum
Terry Rapson	Ian Holm
Vice-Pres. Becker	Kenneth Welsh
Dr Lucy Hall	Sela Ward
Jason Evans	Dash Mihok
J.D.	Austin Nichols
US-President Blake	Perry King
Brian Parks	Arjay Smith
Janet Tokada	Tamlyn Tomita
Parker	Sasha Roiz
Luther	Glenn Plummer
Frank Harris	Jay O. Sanders

Chapters

1 Giving way
2 UN conference
3 A big drop
4 Old wounds
5 A bumpy ride
6 Bad omens
7 The decathlon
8 Too fast
9 LA
10 Worst-case scenario
11 Mountain of data
12 New York City
13 Wall of water
14 The new ice age
15 Contact
16 Presidential briefing
17 A toast
18 Life or death
19 North and south
20 Hard choices
21 Warming up
22 Good friend gone
23 The age of reason
24 Passing the torch
25 The view from space
26 Aboard the ship
27 Eye of the storm
28 Promises to keep
29 The last mile
30 Moving forward
31 End credits

Bei den *post-viewing activities* im letzten Teil des Arbeitsheftes geht es um die Rezeption des Films. Der Regisseur Roland Emmerich kommt hier zu Wort, ebenso ein Wissenschaftler, der direkte Kritik am Film äußert. Des Weiteren gilt es hier, eine klassische Filmkritik zu analysieren. Und schließlich geht es um Ihre Stellungnahme zu *global warming* und zur Präsentation dieses Problems.

Schließlich noch ein Hinweis: Bei der Beschäftigung mit dem Film empfehlen wir die Arbeit mit einem *viewing log*. Wahrscheinlich haben Sie Erfahrung mit der Nutzung eines *reading log* beim Umgang mit komplexen Texten. Bei der Filmanalyse ist es besonders notwendig, beim Anschauen des Films Informationen zu speichern, da es hier viel umständlicher ist „zurückzublättern" wie in einem Buch. Praktische Hinweise zu ▸ *Working with a film viewing log* finden Sie ebenfalls unter www.cornelsen.de/abi-e. Unter dieser Adresse finden Sie auch Hinweise zu ▸ *How to write a film review* sowie Lösungen bzw. Lösungsvorschläge zu einzelnen Aufgaben im Heft, die Sie bei Bedarf abrufen und für sich prüfen können.

Wir wünschen Ihnen gutes Gelingen und viel Erfolg bei der Arbeit am Film und mit diesem Arbeitsheft.

Christina Diehr

Cordula Rohlmann-Reineke

The plot

Jack Hall, a climatologist, is on an expedition in Antarctica with two colleagues, Frank and Jason, when their ice shelf breaks off from the rest of the continent. Jack presents his findings on global warming and a new ice age due to the disrupted North Atlantic current at a United Nations conference, but the diplomats, including the Vice-President of the United States, are not convinced by Jack's theory.

However, Jack's concerns resonate with Professor Terry Rapson of the Hedland Climate Research Centre in Scotland. When two buoys in the North Atlantic simultaneously show a massive drop in the ocean temperature, Rapson concludes that melting of the polar ice has begun disrupting the North Atlantic current.

All over the world violent weather causes mass destruction, including a snowstorm, a hailstorm and an outbreak of tornadoes destroying Los Angeles. The situation worsens when three massive hurricane-like blizzard superstorms begin to form over the northern hemisphere, with their eyes pulling down super-cooled air that causes anything in contact with it to instantly freeze, thus heralding the predicted ice age in seven to ten days.

At the same time Jack's son Sam is in New York City for an academic competition with his friends Brian and Laura, where they also befriend a student named JD. During the competition, the weather becomes massively violent with an intense wind and flooding rains. As the storm worsens in Manhattan, a tidal wave of overwhelming size hits the island, causing major flooding. Sam and his friends are able to seek refuge in the New York Public Library.

The President orders the evacuation of the southern half of the country, while Jack sets off for Manhattan to find his son, accompanied by Jason and Frank, who dies as the result of an accident. The US President's motorcade is fatally caught in the superstorm, leaving the Vice-President in charge.

Inside the library, Sam advises everyone of his father's instruction to stay indoors, but very few listen. Laura becomes severely ill so Sam, Brian, and JD search for penicillin in a cargo ship that has drifted inland and are attacked by wolves escaped from the zoo. The eye of the superstorm begins to pass over the city with its –150 °F (–101 °C) temperatures, and the entire New York City skyline begins to freeze. The three return to the library with necessary supplies like medicine and food.

After the deep freeze, Jack and Jason resume their journey, finally arriving in New York City. They find the library and thus Sam's group alive and are rescued. The new President orders search and rescue teams to look for other survivors. The film ends showing most of the northern hemisphere covered in ice.

Questions on the film

After having read the plot summary you now have an idea of what the film is about. Consider the following questions taking in the light of your knowledge of the film so far and your expectations.

- What do you expect of a film with the title *The Day After Tomorrow*?
- Imagine you were the director. Which actors and actresses would you cast for the main roles and why?
- As a marketing director how would you advertise the film and who would be your target group?
- Why do think is this film was made a topic for *Zentralabitur*?
- What aspects of the film are you particularly interested in?
- What do you think your teacher is interested in?
- Describe your impression of the relationship between father and son.
- Guess why the Vice-President of the US and other diplomats are not convinced by Jack's theory.
- What would you take with you in the case of an evacuation?
- What might happen to Professor Rapson?
- What do you think happens to the people who leave the New York Public library?
- Describe the relationship between Sam, Ryan, JD and Laura.
- Imagine Jack and the new President meet again. What would their relationship be like?
- What do you think is the overall message of a film like this?
- Do you think that a film like this can influence people's attitudes in a lasting way?

Scene index

Chapter (Time)	Characters / Action
	Introduction / Opening credits 0:00:00–0:03:10
0:00:00–0:03:10	Flying over arctic ice shelves, closing in on the research station at Larson B.
1	**Giving way 0:03:11–0:06:24**
0:03:11–0:06:24	At the research station: Jack Hall and his friends/colleagues Frank Harris and Jason Evans are drilling for ice core samples. While doing so first a cleft then an abyss appears in the ice. Jack Hall manages to escape narrowly.
2	**UN conference 0:06:25–0:09:31**
0:06:25–0:08:22	UN conference in Delhi: Jack delivers a talk on the effects of global warming. His conclusion: There will be a new ice age. American-Vice President Becker refutes Jack's assumptions.
0:08:22–0:09:31	It's snowing in New Delhi; Jack is approached by British professor Terry Rapson, who believes that Jack is right.
3	**A big drop 0:09:32–0:12:30**
0:09:32–0:10:58	A buoy shows an extreme drop in the water temperature. Just a malfunction? Prof. Rapson arrives at his research station in Scotland.
0:10:59–0:12:30	Huge hailstones come down on Tokyo.
4	**Old wounds 0:12:31–0:14:42**
0:12:31–0:14:01	In Washington: Jack is back home. Because their son, Sam, has failed a maths class at school, he calls his ex-wife, Dr. Lucy Hall, who is watching a news report about worldwide catastrophes together with Sam.
0:14:02–0:14:42	Jack is warned by his boss not to upset the Vice-President. Jack takes Sam to the airport. Sam participates in a school contest in New York.
5	**A bumpy ride 0:16:01–0:18:54**
0:16:01–0:16:38	On the ISS: warning about a huge storm system.
0:16:39–0:18:54	The plane with Sam and his fellow students Laura Chapman and Brian Parks hits hard weather.
6	**Bad omens 0:18:55–0:21:04**
0:18:55–0:20:01	At the research station in Scotland: More buoys show a dramatic decrease in water temperature.
0:20:02–0:21:04	Sam and his friends have arrived in NY. Birds leave NY; animals in the zoo become very nervous.
7	**The decathlon 0:21:05–0:22:50**
0:21:05–0:21:47	At the school contest: Jack and his team participate successfully.
0:21:48–0:22:50	At a party, JD – a boy from a NY school – shows Laura around.
8	**Too fast 0:22:51–0:24:08**
0:22:51–0:24:08	Prof. Rapson calls Jack in Washington to talk about the weather changes. Prof. Rapson believes that the sudden change of climate Jack has alluded to at the UN conference is happening right now.

Chapter (Time)	Characters / Action
9	**LA 0:24:09–0:31:31**
0:24:09–0:24:32	In the suburbs of Los Angeles the wind is increasing. Bad weather is approaching.
0:24:33–0:25:26	At an LA weather station a whirlwind can be observed.
0:25:27–0:26:11	Extreme weather prediction for LA.
0:26:12–0:27:01	In Washington Jack tries to convince his boss of the necessity to observe the weather changes.
0:27:02–0:30:49	Several tornadoes hit LA, which is eventually devastated.
0:30:50–0:31:31	The Vice-President informs President Blake; air traffic is suspended.
10	**Worst-case scenario 0:31:32–0:37:52**
0:31:32–0:33:45	At a crisis meeting, different explanations for world-wide weather phenomena are discussed, Jack proposes changes in the North Atlantic Current.
0:33:46–0:34:27	Jack's ex-wife is working in an oncologic children's ward, taking special care of an ill boy.
0:34:28–0:35:35	Computer simulations show there will be a new Ice Age in about 16 weeks.
0:35:36–0:36:29	Sam calls his dad to tell him that he will not come home that day but stay at JD's.
0:36:30–0:37:27	Jack tries to convince the Vice President of his theory.
0:37:28–0:37:52	Sam and some other students visit the Museum of Natural History.
11	**Mountain of data 0:37:53–0:41:49**
0:37:53–0:40:57	In Scotland: Helicopters trying to evacuate the Royal Family crash down; one of the pilots freezes to death immediately.
0:40:58–0:41:49	Prof. Rapson asks Jack for help in order to analyze all the data they have got.
12	**Revenge 0:41:50–0:47:35**
0:41:50–0:42:38	In New York City: Jack and his fellow students arrive at JD's. Rain is pouring down.
0:42:39–0:44:35	Because of the rain trains are also suspended; sea levels are rising. Sam and his friends are watching the natural devastations on TV. They decide to leave the flat in order to get out of NY.
0:44:36–0:45:14	New York City is flooded; wolves have escaped from the zoo.
0:45:15–0:47:35	The water is high in the streets; people are trying to find shelter. Laura cuts herself while trying to get to the Public Library.
13	**Wall of water 0:47:36–0:50:53**
0:47:36–0:48:00	A wall of water is approaching New York City.
0:48:01–0:49:30	People are seeking shelter at the Public Library. Laura tries to help a woman while the wave has already flooded parts of NY
0:49:31–0:50:53	New York City is completely flooded.
14	**The new ice age 0:50:54–0:53:18**
0:50:54–0:53:18	In Scotland: Prof. Rapson calls Jack. In 7 to 8 days there will be a new ice age.
15	**Contact 0:53:19–1:01:59**
0:53:19–0:57:53	In the NY Public Library: No electricity; mobiles do not work any longer, but Sam is still able to contact his parents via landline. Jack tells his son not to go outside. Sam almost drowns.

Chapter (Time)	Characters / Action
0:57:54–0:59:22	Jack decides to walk to New York City in order to rescue his son. He is asked to first inform the President.
0:59:23–1:01:59	A ship is floating through the streets of NY.
16	**Presidential briefing 1:01:00–1:03:58**
1:01:00–1:03:58	Jack tells the President to evacuate everybody south of a certain line; the President orders the evacuation of all southern states.
17	**A toast 1:03:59–1:05:26**
1:03:59–1:05:26	In Scotland: the scientists around Prof. Rapson face the fact that they will freeze to death because they have run out of fuel for their generator.
18	**Life or death 1:05:27–1:08:29**
1:05:27–1:08:29	In the NY Public Library: people want to leave the library in order to find better shelter. Sam tries to warn them to stay inside.
19	**North and south 1:08:30–1:10:44**
1:08:30–1:09:15	The hospital where Lucy works is being evacuated. As there is no ambulance for the sick boy, Lucy decides to stay.
1:09:16–1:10:13	On his way to New York City Jack is accompanied by his friends Frank and Jason.
1:10:14–1:10:44	Mexico closes its borders with the US. Americans cross the Rio Grande.
20	**Hard choices 1:10:45–1:14:15**
1:10:45–1:11:57	In the NY Public Library. A small group has remained in the library. They are burning books in order to keep warm.
1:11:58–1:13:28	In the hospital. The hospital is being evacuated. Lucy stays with the sick boy.
1:13:29–1:14:15	Brian hears of the evacuation order on the radio.
21	**Warming up 1:14:15–1:16:46**
1:14:16–1:15:01	Jack and his friends are on their way to New York City: after a car crash they have to walk.
1:15:02–1:16:46	The people who have left the library are trying to keep warm outside. Some have already died. Inside the library the others are also trying to keep warm.
22	**A good friend gone 1:16:47–1:19:50**
1:16:47–1:19:50	Jack and his friends unknowingly walk on the glass roof of a shopping mall. Crashing through the glass Frank cuts himself off the rope which ties the group together thus saving Jack's and Jason's lives.
23	**The age of reason 1:19:51–1:23:06**
1:19:51–1:20:42	In the library, some books are spared from being burned in order to save some part of civilization; Laura has got a temperature.
1:20:43–1:21:16	Lucy and the boy are finally picked up by an ambulance.
1:21:17–1:23:06	Laura feels unwell.
24	**Passing the torch 1:23:07–1:24:43**
1:23:07–1:24:43	The President's motorcade is caught in the storm with the President being killed. The Vice-President is now in charge.
25	**The view from space 1:24:44–1:27:19**
1:24:44–1:25:55	Laura is very ill. Her cut has become infected, she needs penicillin.

Chapter (Time)	Characters / Action
1:25:56–1:27:19	From space the ISS tells NASA that there will be a super-tornado that is going to hit New York City in about an hour.
26	**Aboard the ship 1:27:20–1:33:40**
1:27:20–1:31:24	Sam wants to find medicine for Laura aboard a ship. Brian and JD come along. Meanwhile a pack of wolves looking for food also come aboard the ship. After having found penicillin and food Brian is attacked by a wolf.
1:31:25–1:31:45	Satellite pictures show that the eye of the superstorm is just above New York City.
1:31:46–1:33:40	Sam distracts the wolves so that the boys can escape.
27	**Eye of the storm 1:33:39–1:36:26**
1:33:39–1:36:26	Jack – still on his way to New York City – notices that he and Jason are just in the eye of the storm. They make it to a safe shelter. At the same time: All of New York City is shock-freezing. The boys make it to the library, which completely freezes up.
28	**Promises to keep 1:36:27–1:41:22**
1:36:27–1:40:02	The eye of the storm has passed. Jack and Jason continue their hike to New York City. They reach Staten Island and find many dead bodies.
1:40:03–1:40:35	From the ISS one can see that the northern hemisphere is practically covered by ice, but the storm is clearing.
1:40:36–1:41:22	The next morning Jack and Jason wake up to a blue sky and sunshine.
29	**The last mile 1:41:23-1:44.57**
1:41:23-1:44.57	Seeing the frozen (but still standing) Statue of Liberty, Jack and Jason reach Manhattan. They find the library, which is totally covered by snow and ice. They enter and start looking for Sam, who they finally find in the room where he and a few others have taken refuge.
30	**Moving forward 1:44:58–1:49:27**
1:44:58–1:46:42	The new President is informed that Jack has made it to New York City and that there are some survivors. From an embassy in a Third World country he delivers a speech that is transmitted all over the world.
1:46:43–1:48:58	Helicopters are flying around New York City looking for survivors.
1:48:59–1:49:27	From the ISS one can see that all pollution has gone.
	End Titles 1:49:28–1:58:35

Winter – Approaching the topic of the film

- What does *winter* mean? Make a mind map on the topic.

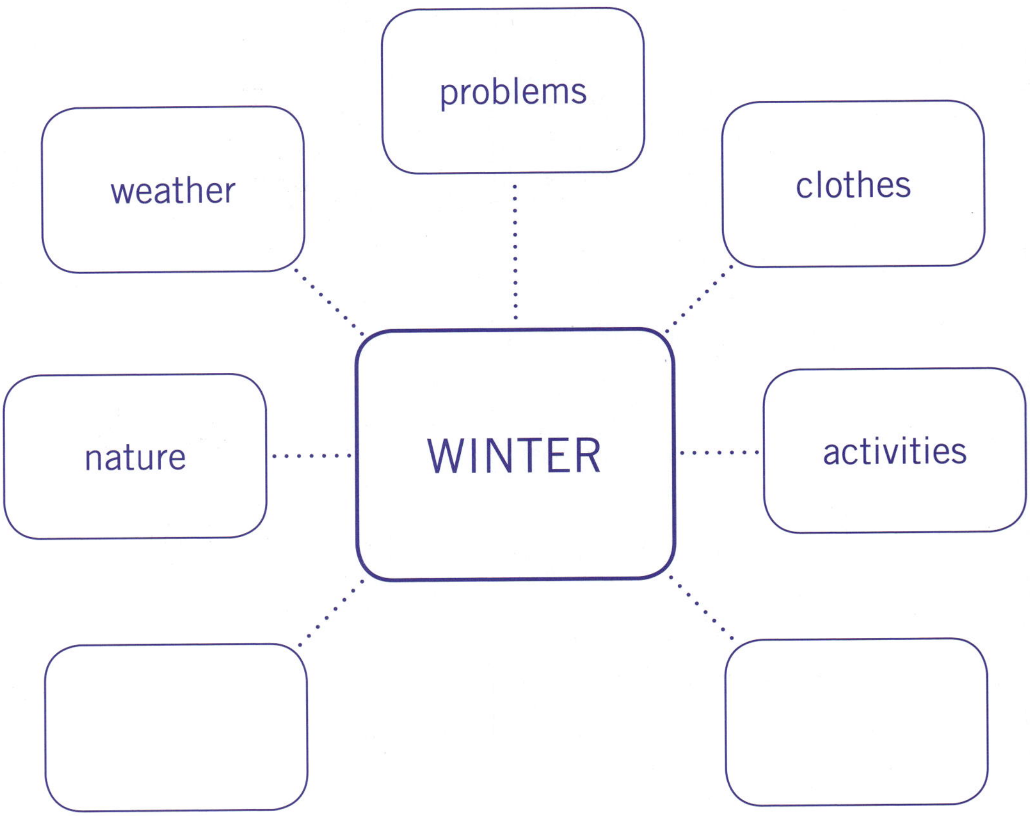

'The Day After Tomorrow' – DVD covers

More cover motifs you can find under:
http://www.amazon.de/Day-After-Tomorrow-Ultimate/dp/B0009A48KO/ref=sr_1_5?s=dvd&ie=UTF8&qid=1284738792&sr=1-5
http://ecx.images-amazon.com/images/I/51vPol8HIML._SL500_AA300_.jpg
http://ecx.images-amazon.com/images/I/51Xw9QwBPTL._SX500_.jpg

■ **1** Film corporations have used different covers for the DVD. Have a closer look at some of the covers.

■ **2** Compare the covers. What are the main differences?

■ **3** What is put in the foreground? What effect on the public does this aim at?

■ **4** Which cover do you prefer? Give reasons for your answer.

The film genre

Main Film Genres		Film Sub-Genres	
	Action Films		Biographical Films (or 'Biopics')
	Adventure Films		'Chick' Flicks
	Comedy Films		Detective & Mystery Films
	Crime & Gangster Films		Disaster Films
	Drama Films		Fantasy Films
	Epics / Historical Films		Film Noir
	Horror Films		Guy Films
	Musical (Dance) Films		Melodramas, Women's or 'Wheeper' Films
	Science Fiction Films		Road Films
	War (Anti-War) Films		Romance Films
	Westerns		Sports Films
			Supernatural Films
			Thriller Suspense Films

INFO

Film Genres

Film genres are various forms or identifiable types, categories, classifications or groups of films that have similar, familiar or instantly-recognizable patterns, filmic techniques or conventions – that include one or more of the following: settings (and props), content and subject matter, themes, mood, period, plot, motifs, styles, structures, situations, recurring icons (e.g., six-guns and ten-gallon hats in Westerns), stock characters (or characterizations) and stars. Many films are considered hybrids – they cover several film genres.

From: http://www.filmsite.org/filmgenres.html

■ 1 Take a look at the list of main film genres and sub-genres.

■ 2 Collect examples of films you know that belong to a main or sub-genre and exchange your filmic experiences.

■ 3 What genre is your favourite? What about your friends? And your parents?

■ 4 What genre do you think *The Day After Tomorrow* belongs to?

■ 5 *Creative writing:* Think up a concept for a successful disaster film. First write down the 'ingredients' you need. Then describe what you want to do with these ingredients.

Approaching the characters

0:35:32

1:06:00

0:08:02

0:58:13

0:21:46

0:53:55

■ **1** In a first step write down your impression of the characters.

■ **2** What relationships do you think are probable between these characters? Draw lines between them and use symbols and key-words to describe their relations.

■ **3** Compare your findings with those of a partner. Decide on one version and then compare it with the version of another team.

The Hall family

■ 1 Take a look at these stills. What do they reveal about the Halls' family life?

Watch the sequence [0:13:00–0:14:01]

▸ Don't forget to start your *viewing log* (www.cornelsen.de/abi-e) to keep track of the film as well as of striking devices.

0:14:00

0:13:49

■ 2 Add new aspects to your characterization of the Halls.

■ 3 Prepare a one-minute talk titled *The Halls.*

■ 4 *Creative writing:* Choose one of the characters from the sequence you have just watched and write his/her diary entry for the day.

0:13:27

The father-son relationship

First impressions

Watch sequence [0:14:40–0:16:00]

■ 1 Make notes in your ▸ *viewing log* / in a grid of the contents and the filmic devices. If you are not sure about the different filmic devices check ▸ *Selected terms for film analysis* under www.cornelsen.de/abi-e

Time code	Contents	Filmic devices

■ 2 Find out more about the father-son relationship by taking a closer look at the different stages of the conversation. Note down your observations.

■ 3 Now analyse the atmosphere in the car. How is this atmosphere created with filmic devices?

■ 4 How do Jack and Sam feel at the end of this sequence?

Development of the father-son relationship

■ 1 After having watched sequence [0:14:40–0:16:00] trace the development of the father-son relationship. Work together with a partner. Partner A focuses on Jack, partner B on Sam.

It is advisable to make a chart in your ▸ *viewing log*.

Watch these sequences: [0:55:13–0:57:22] [1:06:08–1:08:08] [1:16:08–1:16:43] [1:38:46–1:40:02]

■ 2 What can you find out about the feelings 'your' character has for your partner's? What actions derive from these feelings?

■ 3 Exchange and compare your findings.

■ 4 Pair up with another team and exchange your results.

■ 5 In this group discuss if the relationship has changed. If so, to what extent? If not, what accounts for the problems at the beginning?

It's not time to make a change
Cat Stevens

Just relax, take it easy
You're still young, that's your fault,
There's so much you have to know
Find a girl, settle down, if you want you can marry
Look at me, I am old but I'm happy

I was once like you are now
And I know that it's not easy
To be calm when you've found something going on
But take your time, think a lot, why think of everything you've got
For you will still be here tomorrow but your dreams may not

How can I try to explain, 'cos when I do he turns away again
It's always been the same, same old story
From the moment I could talk, I was ordered to listen
Now there's a way and I know that I have to go away
I know, I have to go

(*Instrumental*)

It's not time to make a change,
Just sit down take it slowly
You're still young, that's your fault,
There's so much you have to go through
Find a girl, settle down, if you want you can marry
Look at me, I am old but I'm happy

All the times that I've cried keeping all the things I knew inside
It's hard, but it's harder to ignore it
If they were right I'd agree, but it's them they know, not me
Now there's a way and I know that I have to go away
I know, I have to go

■ **1** Describe what the song is about.

■ **2** Analyse who says what and what the relationship between the two people is like.

■ **3** What parallels and differences do you see between the relationships described in the film and in this song?

A closer look at some minor characters

INFO

Minor character
A minor character is any character in your story that is not a major character. Minor characters have many important roles in a story. They can move the plot along, provide conflict, or serve as part of the setting. They can be foils for the major characters. A foil serves to highlight the characteristics of protagonists for the reader [viewer] by comparison and contrast. You do not usually need to develop your minor characters as fully as your major characters, but, depending on how important they are to the progress of the story, you should pay some attention to developing them.

http://www.ehow.com/how_4545852_create-minor-character-fiction.html

0:20:13

★
Luther Just another typical day in New York City. Traffic jam ten blocks long! Lookie here, Buddha. These people, and their cars, and their exhaust, and they're just polluting the atmosphere!

★
Laura You live here?
JD Just on the weekends.

0:42:15

■ **1** Analyse the composition of the two stills. What do viewers get to see? What is the effect of this?

■ **2** What role do the two characters depicted in the stills play in the film?

■ **3** Explain their function in the film.

■ **4** *Creative writing:* Write a new sequence for the film: A meeting between Luther and JD one week before the catastrophe. The sequence should not be longer than 30 seconds.

▸ If you need information on how to write a film script, watch the video on
http://www.5min.com/Video/How-to-Write-a-Script-14073221
or find a sample script at
http://extras.timesonline.co.uk/samplescript.pdf

Luther and JD are two characters that – under normal circumstances – would never get in contact with each other. Because of the catastrophe they are now confined together in the library.

★
JD What are you doing?
Luther Insulating. Newspaper's best, but this'll do. You know you spend some years on the streets and you learn how to keep warm. ... Hey (*throws a book at JD*) ...
JD Thanks.

1:15:53

■ **5** Take a look at these two stills and analyse them with regard to filmic devices.

■ **6** First explain what the stills reveal about the relationship between the two characters and then consider their conversation.

■ **7** Is the function of the two characters for the film the same as before? Justify your opinion.

1:16:03

1:19:56

Another 'set' of minor characters are the librarian and the girl who have decided to stay in the library together with Sam.

1:20:06

■ **8** First take a look at the stills and then describe the two characters.

■ **9** Next read the dialogue and describe the function these two characters have for the film.

★

Girl What have you got there?
Librarian A Gutenberg Bible. It was in the rare books room.
Girl You think God's gonna save you?
Librarian No. I don't believe in God.
Girl You're holding onto that Bible pretty tight.
Librarian I'm protecting it. This Bible is the first book ever printed. It represents the dawn of the age of reason. As far as I'm concerned, the written word is man's greatest achievement. You can laugh. But if Western civilization is finished I'm gonna save at least a little piece of it.

1:48:18

■ **10** Finally have a look at this still and add new aspects to the function of the two characters.

■ **11** Imagine the director had cut out Luther, JD, the librarian and the girl. What would be the consequences? Think of single (major) characters, but also of the plot and the message the film wants to convey. Fill in a chart completing the if-clauses.

If the director had cut out …

… Luther …	
… JD …	
… the librarian …	
… the girl …	

The creation of suspense

As *The Day After Tomorrow* is a science-fiction disaster film, creating suspense is one of the main 'ingredients' for a successful film.

- **1** What are the main filmic techniques used to create suspense?
- **2** Make a mind map and be prepared to present it.

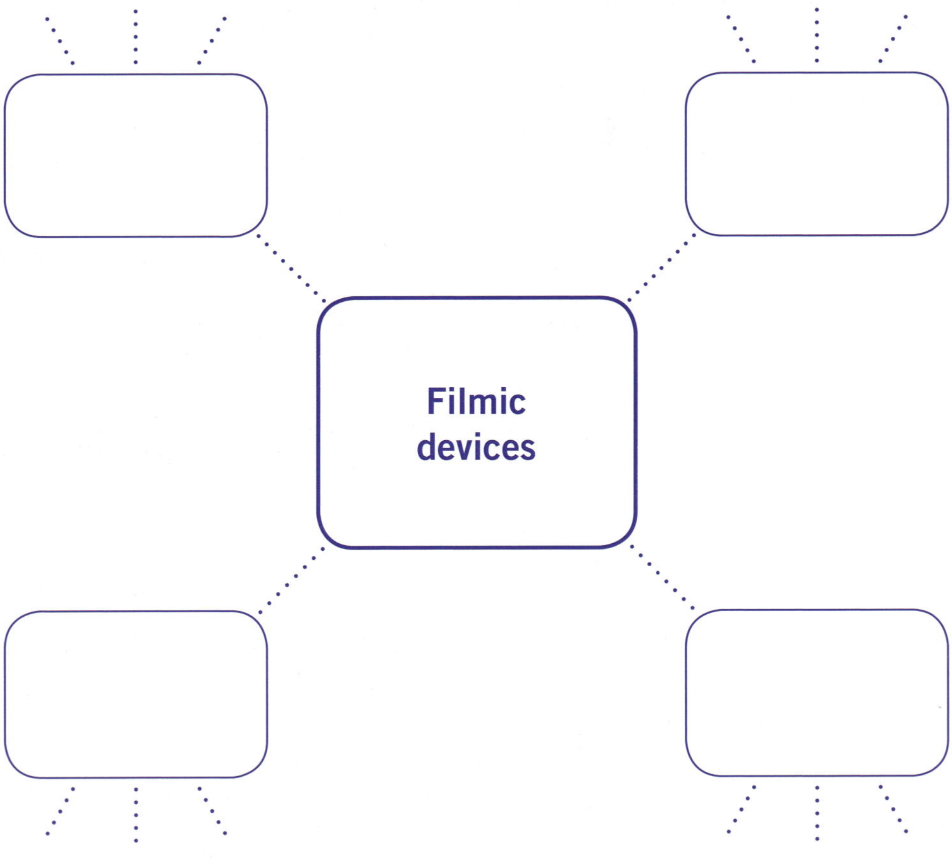

How is suspense created in 'The Day After Tomorrow'?

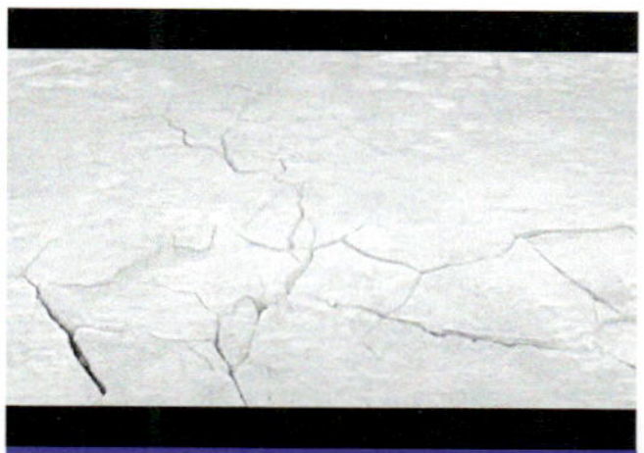
0:03:48

0:05:15

0:06:03

0:21:46

1:08:56

1:34:01

■ **1** Look at these stills and relate them to aspects of suspense.

■ **2** Exchange your findings. From your point of view what are the most effective means of creating suspense as used in the stills?

1:36:22

Move on to a larger scale, namely the analysis of sequences:

Watch sequences [0:27:37–0:29:19] [1:17:35–1:20:10] [1:36:24–1:37:22]

▸ Note your results in your *viewing log*.

■ **3** Watch these sequences twice (or even more often) and analyse them as to the creation of suspense.

■ **4** Again exchange your findings. What are the most effective means of creating suspense in the sequences you have watched?

■ **5** Summarize your results. Make a top-five list of the most effective means of creating suspense.

Aspects of patriotism

The Day After Tomorrow does not only focus on natural disasters and their consequences on mankind, but also on mankind's struggle to survive in an unfriendly and potentially deadly environment. Can you imagine that in times of trouble a nation's 'character' is called upon to ensure survival? In this context patriotism is an important key word.

■ **1** What is patriotism?

■ **2** Discuss: Do you see differences between Germans and Americans in their attitude towards patriotism?

■ **3** Have a close look at these stills. What filmic techniques are used? Relate the stills to aspects of patriotism.

0:03:00

0:26:10

0:46:10

1:35:00

1:36:22

1:42:35

1:43:23

■ **4** What aspects of patriotism can you find in the speech?

■ **5** What are the filmic devices used to present the President's speech in the film?

■ **6** What is the overall message of this speech?

■ **7** Do you think this speech is convincing? Give reasons for your answer.

Take a look at President Becker's speech [1:47:07–1:49:06].

'The Day After Tomorrow' – Interview with Roland Emmerich

Roland Emmerich has directed some of the biggest movies in the history of Hollywood. His surprise hit *Stargate* took off in 1994, and was quickly followed by *Independence Day*, the event movie to end them all. After stumbling with the 1998 remake *Godzilla*, Emmerich made a proud return to form with the period epic *The Patriot*, and this week returns to theatre screens nationwide with the disaster epic *The Day After Tomorrow*, about a catastrophic change in the world's climate due to global warming. Emmerich sat down with blackfilm.com to discuss the scientific possibilities of his latest opus, as well as maintaining a career as a director whose filmography eclipses even those of the biggest moviemakers in the industry.

Can you discuss the controversy this film has raised over the possibility of global warming's effects on the environment?

RE: I'm a film maker, not a scientist. But I had a very smart and intelligent screenwriter, who did a lot of research, and he tried to keep it as accurate as possible.

Could it really happen in eight days?

RE: No, that's pure fiction. But global warming leads to another ice age. That's happened before, so we know that.

What's the attraction for you of tearing down cities?

RE: I knew this question would come when I do this movie, but I felt it was such an important thing to do, that I, because of that reason, did it again. After *Independence Day* I didn't want to do it again because I didn't want to repeat myself. But I also thought that this movie is very different from *Independence Day* and all my other movies.

Is it because of the message of the movie?

RE: Yeah, exactly. When you find something where you can give people a message and still make it an exciting movie, you get very, very excited about something. You probably even work harder than you normally do.

Was it because of this environmental message that the movie is more serious than your previous films?

RE: Yeah. I couldn't see the same kind of tongue-in-cheek humour. That's like aliens, and the movie didn't have to take itself so seriously.

5 *period epic* a long film about a certain period of time in the past
9 *opus* important piece of work
32 *tongue-in-cheek humour* joking

This movie has some humor too, but it's a little more subversive, it's a little more hidden.

Was the tidal wave sequence in New York the biggest challenge?

RE: We were very sensitive. For instance, if that much water hit the Statue of Liberty, it would crumble, but in our movie it still stands. For me it's a symbol that a lot has changed. There's not really much destruction in New York besides the weather and it's a natural force so it's not like any destruction. But LA gets leveled (laughs). That's my comment to Hollywood.

What about Americans crossing the border into Mexico?

RE: Well, that's what interested me about it. I was really surprised when I read that global warming can lead to another ice age. Everybody knows that the industrialized nations are the worst offenders. Europe and North America catch their warmth from the Gulf Stream, so if this Gulf Stream shuts down, we will have an ice age in Europe and America that means that we cannot live here anymore. Everybody has to go south. Because it's an American movie, I thought, 'okay, great, they have to all go to Mexico – what will Mexico do?' Again, it's a little bit of a Utopia, we had a scene in there which we cut out that you will see on the DVD where the Vice-President comes storming into the Oval Office and says, 'the Mexicans have closed the border. We can open it by force if we want to!' And we cut it out because we thought that, in a situation like that, this would not happen, it would be more like: how can we deal with the fact that this is happening? It's a little like Sept. 11, the whole world in a way was one.

How political were you trying to get with a president and a vice-president that, at least visually, referenced Bush and Cheney?

RE: Well, when you make a movie about global warming causing a new ice age that takes place in America, you have to portray a government. If you want to make it real you have to portray somewhat the political government which is in place right now. And it's a fact that they kind of don't do anything for the environment. They think it's all a big hoax.

You also took a shot at Cheney, with the President deferring to the Vice-President all the time ...

RE: Well, (*laughs*) think whatever you want. I'm only a stupid film maker (*laughs*).

Are you hoping this movie will create a discussion about the environment?

34 *subversive* indirect
51 *Utopia* imaginary place in which everything is perfect
59 *Bush* 43th President of the USA (2001–2009) *Cheney* 46th Vice-President of the USA (2001–2009)
64 *hoax* an act intended to make sb believe sth that is not true
65 *defer to* agree to accept what sb has decided

RE: I hope it creates discussion. It already created discussion, you know what I mean? All of a sudden every newspaper, you're like, 'Look, there's some guy from the right wing saying it's all fucking bullshit.' And then some environmentalist says, 'No it's not. Global warming is real.' And it's already caused so much noise that I think I already accomplished it. There's already so much out there. And me talking here about it, you guys filter the results to the audience and everything. It doesn't really matter if this movie is a success or not, because it's already out there. In one respect, it's also really interesting, because all the newspapers in Europe always make a part that's the film, and then the next side was the real science, the real danger. That's like amazing about it. I think we are obsessed with entertainment. The whole Western world is obsessed with entertainment. I don't know about the Third World really; maybe they are too. It's like everybody is obsessed with Hollywood movies worldwide. And even though everybody hates the Americans, they're still watching American movies. So, in that way, entertainment can do much more than, probably, a book or article.

74 *accomplish* succeed in doing sth

Todd Gilchrist, May 2004:
http://webcache.googleusercontent.com/search?q=cache:pbJP5Q9gC-4J:www.blackfilm.com/20040528/features/rolandemmerich.shtml+%22Are+you+hoping+this+movie+will+create%22+Emmerich&cd=1&hl=de&ct=clnk&gl=de&client=firefox-a

1 Reading for gist

Which statement sums up the main idea of the text:

a *The Day After Tomorrow* mainly deals with criticism of governments being too passive and ignorant politicians.
b The film is mainly about a father-son relationship.
c The film mainly deals with the negative effects of global warming.

2 Reading for detail

Finish the sentence by choosing the correct ending:

In his movie Roland Emmerich
a gives an accurate scientific scenario of the effects of global warming.
b does not focus on scientific aspects at all.
c shows the negative impact of global warming.

Roland Emmerich thinks that *The Day After Tomorrow* is
a comparable to his other films.
b completely different from his other films.
c a copy of his other films.

The Day After Tomorrow is
a a mere action movie.
b a serious film.
c a mixture of different genres.

According to Emmerich,
a it is no problem at all having parts of NYC destroyed.
b the events of 9/11 kept him from having NYC destroyed completely.
c NYC should not be destroyed completely to create hope.

■ **3** According to Emmerich, why is the movie *The Day After Tomorrow* so special?

■ **4** Explain why film makers are sensitive about having New York City destroyed.

■ **5** Explain why the film makers cut out a scene where the Vice-President comes storming into the Oval Office and says, 'the Mexicans have closed the border. We can open it by force if we want to!' (ll. 52ff.)

■ **6** What do you think: Can movies like *The Day After Tomorrow* create a discussion about the environment? Explain your position.

■ **7** Do film makers have a certain responsibility for showing the truth?
Give reasons for your opinion.

A lot of hot air – A scientist's view

As a scientist, I bristle when lies dressed up as 'science' are used to influence political discourse. The latest example is the global-warming disaster flick, *The Day After Tomorrow*.

This film is propaganda designed to shift the policy of this nation on climate change. At least that's what I take from producer Mark Gordon's comment that 'part of the reason we made this movie' was to 'raise consciousness about the environment.'

Fox spokesman Jeffrey Godsick says, 'The real power of the movie is to raise consciousness on the issue of global warming.'

Oh, the plot. Global warming causes the Gulf Stream to shut down. This current normally brings tropical warmth northward and makes Europe much more comfortable than it should be at its northerly latitude. The heat stays stuck in the tropics, the polar regions get colder, and the atmosphere suddenly flips over in a 'superstorm'. The frigid stratosphere trades places with our habitable troposphere, and in a matter of days, an ice age ensues. Temperatures drop 100 degrees an hour in Canada. Hurricanes ravage Belfast. Folks in Japan are clobbered by bowling-ball-size hailstones. If we had only listened to concerned scientists and stopped global warming when we could.

Each one of these phenomena is physically impossible.

Start with the Gulf Stream. Carl Wunsch, a professor of physical oceanography at Massachusetts Institute of Technology, knows more about ocean currents than most anyone. He thinks the nonsense in *The Day After Tomorrow* detracts from the seriousness of the global-warming issue. So he recently wrote in the prestigious science journal *Nature* that the scenario depicted in the movie requires one to 'turn off the wind system, or to stop the Earth's rotation, or both.'

The stratosphere will become the troposphere when all three laws of thermodynamics are repealed. Hailstones can't reach bowling-ball size because their growth is limited by gravity. Hurricanes can't hit Belfast because the intervening island of Ireland would destroy them.

How do I know so much about a movie that isn't out yet? I've seen the promos, and I've read and reviewed the book upon which it is based, The *Coming Global Superstorm* by Art Bell and Whitley Strieber. In Strieber's previous work, *Communion*, he explained that he was told of the Earth's upcoming apocalypse by aliens. And how this knowledge was

1 *bristle* suddenly become very annoyed at what sb. says or does
8 *Fox* one of the six major American film studios
14 *flip over* turn onto the other side or upside down
stratosphere outer part of the air surrounding the Earth
15 *troposphere* lowest portion of the Earth's atmosphere
17 *clobber* hit
29 *thermodynamics* science dealing with the relation between heat and other forms of energy
repeal to be not valid any longer

communicated is much more the purview of an adult website than a family newspaper. What's on the movie's website is worse – nothing but out-and-out distortion.

It also insists that what is depicted on the screen has already started.

'Did you know,' says the site, that there were more tornadoes recorded in May 2003 than in any other month?

I looked up federal tornado statistics, and indeed they're going up, and there was a peak in May 2003. Then I determined the number of radar stations and their type. When our first radar-tracking network was established in the 1960s and '70s, the number of tornadoes rose proportionally, then leveled off until the new Doppler radars came online in 1988. It took a decade to put this system in place, and the number of reported tornadoes went up accordingly.

Then I plotted the number of severe tornadoes. If anything, it's going down. So the flashy Doppler radars are merely detecting more weak storms that cause little, if any, damage.

The website also implies that global warming is making hurricanes worse. Christopher Landsea, the world's most aptly named hurricane scientist, has studied the maximum winds in these storms as measured by aircraft and finds a significant decline.

Global warming? Some scientists think climate change strengthens El Niño, the large atmospheric oscillation responsible for a variety of weather – both good and bad. El Niños are known to rip apart hurricanes. So it's more likely that climate change is weakening these storms than enhancing them.

[...]

Far be it from me to criticize anyone's freedom of expression. But remember that propaganda can have consequences. McCain's and Lieberman's measure mimics the United Nations' infamous Kyoto Protocol on global warming, which many scientists know will do nothing measurable about planetary temperature within the policy-relevant future. But it will cost money.

This isn't Hollywood's first attempt to scare people into its way of thinking.

[...]

37 *purview* within the limits of what a person, an organization is responsible for; dealt with by a document, law, etc. (Geltungsbereich)
39 *out-and-out* in every way
distortion change of facts
57 *El Niño* causes extreme weather such as floods, droughts and other weather disturbances in many regions of the world
58 *oscillation* regular movement of sth. from side to side between two limits

Or how about the 1983 movie *The Day After,* whose purpose was to strengthen the nuclear-freeze movement. It failed.

The Day After Tomorrow is only one more day than *The Day After,* and it deserves the same fate. Lies cloaked as science should never determine how we live our lives.

72 *The Day After* television movie from 1983 which portrays a fictional nuclear war that quickly escalates into a full-scale exchange between the US and the former USSR

P. J. Michaels:
http://www.usatoday.com/news/opinion/editorials/2004-05-24-michaels_x.htm

Patrick J. Michaels is senior fellow in environmental studies at the Cato Institute and author of the book, Meltdown: The Predictable Distortion of Global Warming by Scientists, Politicians and the Media.

■ **1** Outline the author's view on the film.

■ **2** Analyse how Michaels conveys his position by paying special attention to the tone of the text.

■ **3** Comment on the statement:
'Lies cloaked as science should never determine how we live our lives.' (ll. 75f.)

'The Day After Tomorrow' – Film review

In director Roland Emmerich's *Independence Day* (1996), a boffin eventually defeats the space aliens that have wrought explosive havoc all over America (and incidentally the rest of the world) – without provocation. In *Godzilla* (1998), a boffin eventually defeats the giant iguana that has rampaged through New York City's highrise – but the fact that the lizard's mutation was a product of exposure to Pacific nuclear testing hinted that humankind was just reaping what it (or at least what the French) had sown. And now in *The Day After Tomorrow*, there is yet more disaster and destruction on a truly massive scale all over America (and incidentally the rest of the world), only this time the enemy is global warming, the starring boffin is unable to do anything to defeat it, and the blame is placed squarely on the shoulders of Western consumerism and blinkered US governance. In other words, Emmerich's delight in sublime catastrophe may be consistent to the point of repetitiveness, but at least the man is maturing politically.

A sequence of extreme weather conditions (snow in New Delhi, bucket-sized hailstones in Tokyo, spectacular tornadoes in downtown LA) leads palaeoclimatologist Jack Hall (Dennis Quaid) to realise that a new ice age is coming. His son Sam (Jake Gyllenhaal) becomes trapped in New York's Public Library when a tidal wave strikes the city, and is forced to fight rapidly dropping temperatures – and a pack of hungry wolves escaped from the zoo – while Jack and two colleagues attempt the perilous journey from Washington to find him.

The Day After Tomorrow has everything you expect from a disaster movie: personal dramas set against apocalyptic mayhem; lots of scenes set in control rooms (with no-one in control); recognisable public monuments being torn apart/flooded/buried under snow/snapfrozen; and episodes so preposterously daft that you just have to love them, as when Jack feels the need to explain the relationship between the North Atlantic current and the world's climate to a room full of meteorological experts, or when Sam and his friends outrun a towering wall of water (and later a fast-moving cold snap). Silliest of all is the realisation that Jack has undertaken his journey not to save the good burghers of New York, nor even just to save his own son, but rather simply to prove that he can for once keep an appointment – making the final scenes of this film hilariously anticlimactic, as our hero is left with literally nothing to do except grin.

While Emmerich is really only going over visual effects already well covered by films like *Deep Impact*, Twister or even *Meteor*, he comes into his own in battering his viewers with total sensory overload to convey the sheer, overwhelming scale of the devastation. The bass rumble which

1 *boffin* scientist, especially one doing research
2 *havoc* situation in which there is a lot of damage, destruction or confusion
5 *highrise* very tall and having a lot of floors
7 *reap* cut and collect a crop
12 *squarely* directly or exactly
13 *blinkered* not aware of every aspect of a situation; not willing to accept different ideas about sth
sublime extreme
23 *perilous* very dangerous
25 *mayhem* confusion and fear, usually caused by violent behaviour or by some sudden shocking event
27 *snapfrozen* frozen extremely fast
28 *preposterously* completely unreasonable, especially in a way that is shocking or annoying
daft silly, often in a way that is amusing
32 *coldsnap* a sudden short period of very cold weather
33 *burghers* citizens of a particular town
35 *hilarious* funny
39 *batter* hit sb/sth hard many times, especially in a way that causes serious damage
40 *rumble* long deep sound or series of sounds

accompanies the wave rolling through New York is quite simply the most ear-splitting sound ever heard in a cinema, and if the film's cataclysmic, but occasionally ropey, CGI fails to humble you, the soundtrack might just succeed.

It is for its politics, however, that this film is most audacious, as it represents a direct attack on the refusal of the current US administration to reduce greenhouse emissions. Even if it is somewhat simplistic, *The Day After Tomorrow* may have more impact on Bush's stance on the environment than any serious science could, as it terrifies its American viewers into doing something that the British have always enjoyed – talking about the weather.

Movie Gazette, February 26 2004: http://www.movie-gazette.com/762/the-day-after-tomorrow

42 *cataclysmic* cataclysm: sudden disaster or a violent event that causes change, for example a flood or a war
43 *ropey* not in good condition; of bad quality
CGI computer-generated imagery
45 *audacious* willing to take risks or to do sth shocking
48 *stance on* the opinions that sb has about sth and expresses publicly

■ 1 Outline the author's attitude towards the film.

■ 2 Analyse the language and the tone the author employs to make his point.

■ 3 Comment on the statement that this film 'may have more impact on Bush's stance on the environment than any serious science could' (ll. 48f.).

■ 4 Write your own review of *The Day After Tomorrow*.

If you want some help check ▸ How to write a film review under www.cornelsen.de/abi-e

Global Warming – What can be done?

■ **1** Describe the elements of the cartoon. How are the sharks presented?

■ **2** Analyse the message the cartoon wants to convey.

■ **3** Comment on the impact of the cartoon without speech bubble.

■ **4** How does Emmerich in his *film* deal with 'global warming'? How does the *cartoon* deal with it? Point out similarities and differences.

■ **5** What medium would *you* choose to best point up the potential danger of global warming/climate change? Explain your choice.

What can we do against global warming?

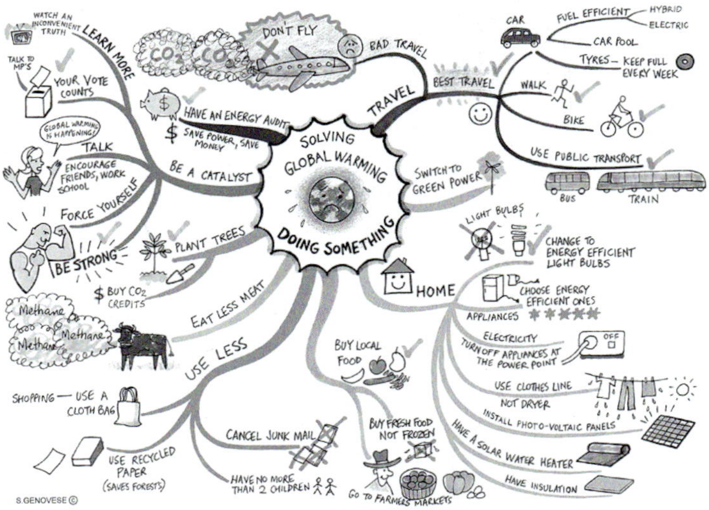

■ **1** Take a look at this mind map. Make a list of aspects you agree with and vice versa.

■ **2** In a group discussion, compare your results with your classmates' findings.

■ **3** Additional task: In a group design a poster by students for students.
Topic: *How to save the Earth.*

Personal responsibility at the dawn of the new ice age

■ Discuss this topic in a fishbowl.

INFO

Fishbowl discussion
A fishbowl discussion is a form of dialogue that can be used when discussing topics within a large group divided into those who form the fishbowl and those who are the 'goldfish'. The advantage of a fishbowl dicussion: it allows the entire group to participate.

There are two different kinds of fishbowl discussions: the *open* and the *closed* fishbowl.

In an open *fishbowl*, one chair is left empty. Any member of the fishbowl can, whenever he/she wants to, sit down on the empty chair and join the 'goldfish' in the inner circle. When this happens, a member of the inner circle must voluntarily leave so that a free chair can again be taken. The discussion continues with participants frequently entering and leaving the inner circle.

In a *closed fishbowl*, all chairs are filled. The moderator introduces the topic and the 'goldfish' start discussing the topic. The audience outside listen to the discussion and take notes. When time runs out all 'goldfish' leave the inner circle and a new group of 'goldfish' from the fishbowl enter.
You can choose whether you want to form an open or a closed fishbowl.

Preparation

■ 1 Decide whether you want to form an open or a closed fishbowl.

■ 2 Divide the class into seven groups.
Groups one to six are responsible for the characters (Jack Hall, Frank Harris, Vice-President Becker, Policeman in Library, Lucy Hall, Prof. Rapson), group seven is responsible for the moderator.

■ 3 Before you start the actual discussion it must be clear who is going to observe whom.

The characters

■ 1 Bearing in mind the topic of the fishbowl discussion write a profile for 'your' character: Who are you? What did you do? What happened to you? Why did you act the way you acted? How did you feel in certain situations? Do you think you did anything wrong?

■ 2 Imagine what 'your' character wants to say to the others. Is he/she thankful/angry/disappointed? Does he/she want to reproach or blame anybody? Does he/she want to justify himself/herself for what he/she has done to somebody else? What does he/she want to ask the others?

The moderator

■ 1 Prepare yourself to …
- welcome the participants of the discussion and explain what the discussion will be about.
- stimulate the discussion by asking the participants questions that 'force' them to take a stance, to explain their motives for certain actions, etc.

■ 2 Explain the rules, namely:
- The goldfish and the members of the fishbowl are not allowed to communicate with each other.
- The goldfish should first introduce themselves: Who are they? What happened to them?
- The goldfish are not allowed to interrupt each other.
- Rules of good behaviour must be followed.

■ 3 Your tasks during the discussion:
- Get the discussion going by calling on one of the participants to start the first round.
- Open the second round by calling on one of the participants to start his/her statement (see topic of discussion).
- Make sure that each goldfish/character is allowed to speak.
- In your role as moderator you must call to order and interrupt participants who do not speak to the topic.
- You are responsible for the flow of the conversation, so be prepared to ask questions (see above).
- At the end of the discussion give a short summary of what the 'goldfish' have said.
- Thank the participants for the discussion.

Evaluation

■ 1 First the participants say how they felt in their role as goldfish.

■ 2 The observers now give feedback to the participants of the discussion. This can be done in small face-to-face teams/groups.

■ 3 For successful feedback it is very important to focus on what somebody did well and then to say what they could do in order to improve their performance.

The following observation sheet can help the observers to give feedback:

Language	**Comment**	**Overall impression (JK)**
Fluency		
Pronunciation/loudness/speed		
Grammar		
Choice of words		
Content		
Substantiality of statements/ answers		
Accordance between statements and character as presented in the film		
Ability to answer questions		
Communication		
Listening to others		
Showing interest in other participants' statements		
Ability to connect one's own ideas to those of the previous speaker		

Topics for upcoming exams

Analysis

Explain the title of the film.
Consider the sequence when the US President delivers his speech about evacuating the northern hemisphere: To what extent do filmic devices such as sound, light, camera work contribute to the mood of this scene?
Analyse Lucy Hall's role as a doctor.
Explain Jack's motives for going to New York City.
Outline Sam's relationship with Laura.
Analyse the (Vice-) President's attitude towards global warming before and after President Blake's death.

Comment

Evaluate Jack's role as a father.
Comment on (Vice-)President Becker's behaviour at the UN Conference in Delhi.
Comment on the ending of the film (the people in the ISS recognize that all pollution is gone). Discuss whether this ending makes sense for you.
Comment on Lucy Hall's staying at the hospital with Peter.
Do you think Jack and Lucy get back together again?
Comment on the impact of disaster films on common people and their attitude towards global warming.

Creative Writing

Frank and Jason decide to accompany Jack to New York City despite the weather conditions. Imagine how they tell their family about their decision. Write a dialogue.
Put yourself into JD's shoes trying to contact his family. Imagine his thoughts after another failed/unanswered call. Write down his interior monologue.
Laura and Sam have a conversation on Sam and Jack's relationship. Write Laura's diary entry.